Enchanted English
Ages 9-10
Alison Head

Aurora is a griffin. She can fly high above the Enchanted Forest and often takes Finn for a ride.

Sparkle, Gem, Dusty and *Firefly* are four playful fairies who live in the bluebell fields.

Professor Willow is a wise old gentleman, who loves to gather facts for his Book of Knowledge.

Gribbit and Periwinkle are naughty pixies who play tricks on the fairies with some help from their bug friends.

Finn is an elf prince, who is mastering the art of living in harmony with nature before he becomes king.

Pearl is a unicorn who lives by the Lake of Wisdom. She loves to travel and shares her stories with the forest creatures.

Welcome to the Enchanted Forest!

Contents

Plurals

I'm Professor Willow. There are several different ways to turn nouns into plurals.

You can often just add **s**, although nouns ending in a hissing, buzzing or shushing sound end in **es**.

Singular nouns ending in **f** usually lose the **f** and add **ves** to become plurals.

If a word ends in a consonant followed by **y**, it loses the **y** and adds **ies** in the plural.

tree**s**   bush**es**   lea**ves**   bab**ies**

1 Circle the correct plurals of these words.

a   wolf   wolves   wolfs

b   loaf   loafs   loaves

c   scarf   scarves   scarfs

d   shelf   shelves   shelfs

e   cuff   cuves   cuffs

f   self   selfs   selves

2 Write down the plurals for these words. Remember to check whether the noun has a consonant before the y.

a   fairy   _____

b   lorry   _____

c   trolley   _____

d   cherry   _____

e   donkey   _____

f   jelly   _____

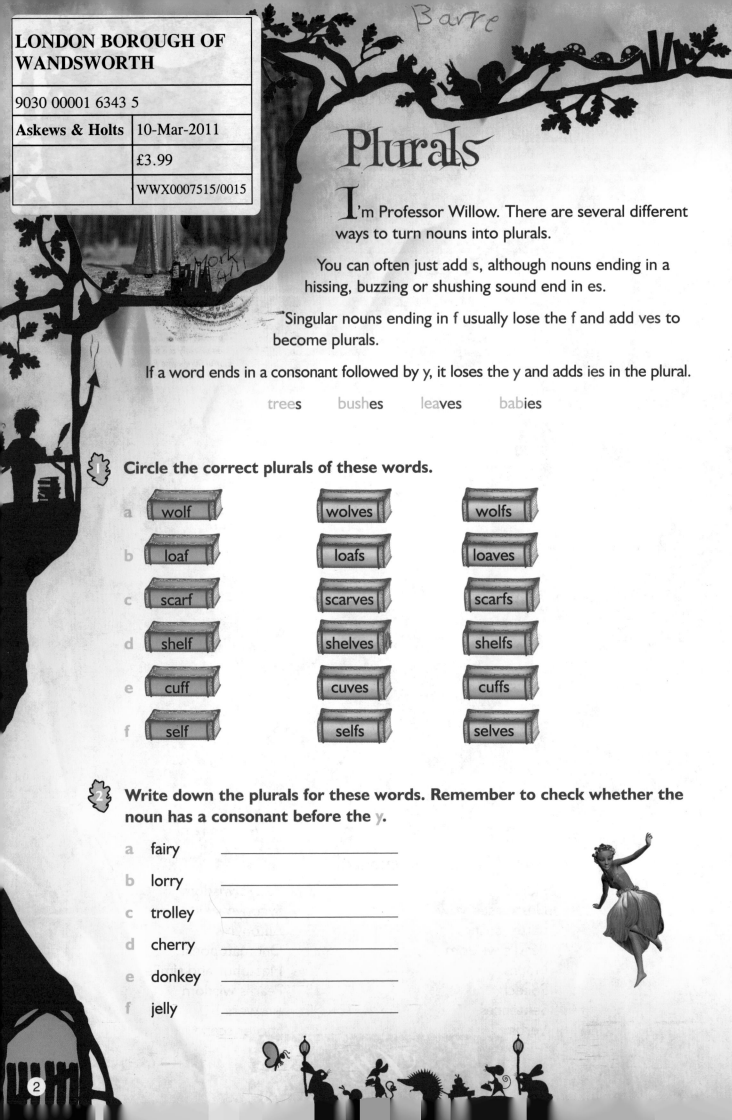

3 Wonderful work! Now change these words into plurals and sort them into the correct boxes, according to how they are made plural.

a owl

b elf

c party

d puppy

e half

f box

g pebble

h dish

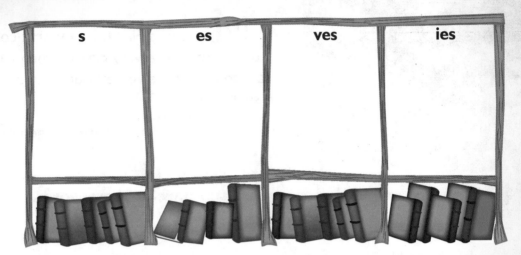

s	es	ves	ies

4 Underline five mistakes in this piece of text.

Everyone in the Enchanted Forest loves it when the pixys organise their magical ball. Each fairy makes wishs for a pretty new dress, with matching glovs made from spiders' webes. Finn polishes Pearl's hoofs until they shine, while Gribbit and Periwinkle pick berrys for the feast.

Willow's Quest

Find the plurals of these nouns in the word search grid.

a worry

b thief

c watch

d city

e calf

a	c	i	t	i	e	s	g
d	w	a	j	y	f	e	w
g	b	x	l	i	k	d	o
e	f	r	h	v	m	l	r
t	h	i	e	v	e	s	r
c	s	q	z	o	n	s	i
t	u	a	b	p	c	h	e
v	w	a	t	c	h	e	s

Find the squirrel and rabbit sticker to add to the map at the back of the book.

Unstressed vowels

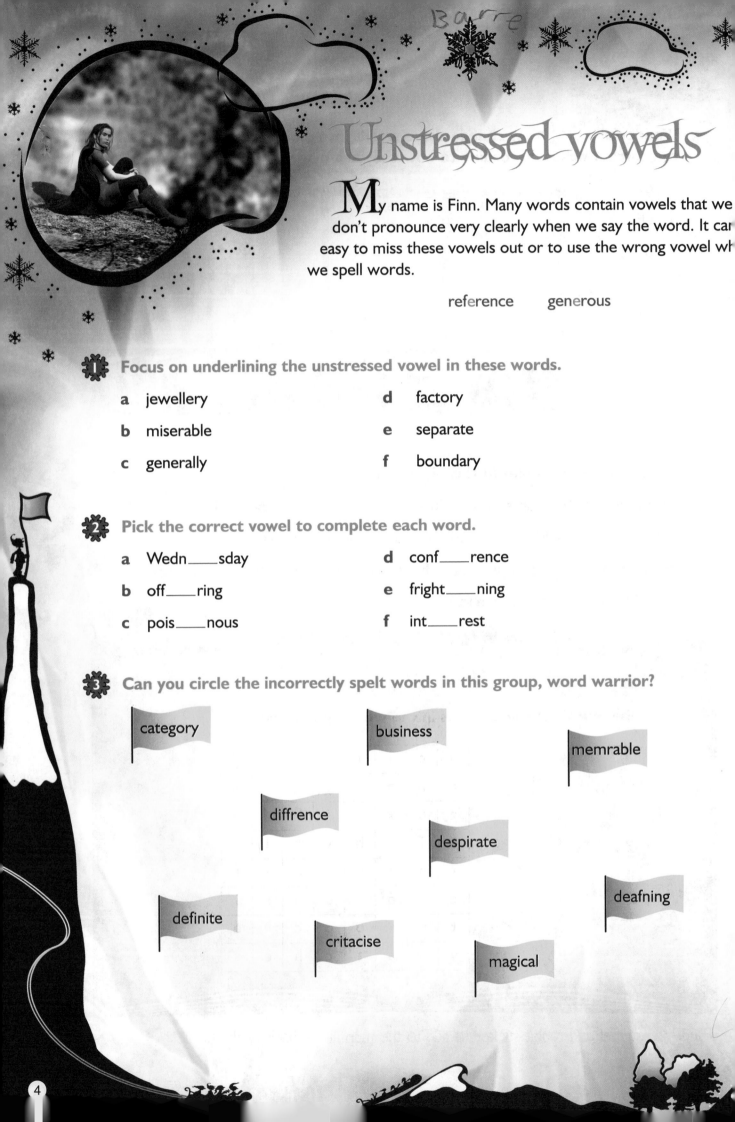

My name is Finn. Many words contain vowels that we don't pronounce very clearly when we say the word. It ca[n] easy to miss these vowels out or to use the wrong vowel wh[en] we spell words.

reference   generous

1 **Focus on underlining the unstressed vowel in these words.**

a   jewellery

b   miserable

c   generally

d   factory

e   separate

f   boundary

2 **Pick the correct vowel to complete each word.**

a   Wedn____sday

b   off____ring

c   pois____nous

d   conf____rence

e   fright____ning

f   int____rest

3 **Can you circle the incorrectly spelt words in this group, word warrior?**

category

business

memrable

diffrence

despirate

deafning

definite

critacise

magical

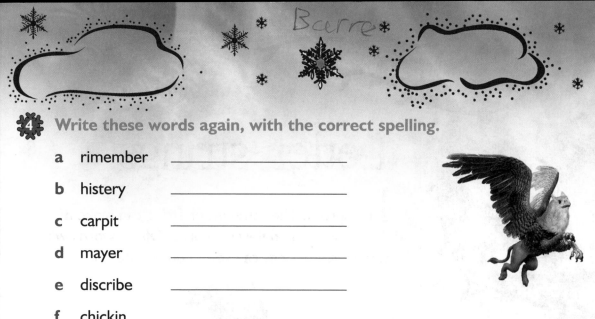

Barre

4 Write these words again, with the correct spelling.

a   rimember   _____

b   histery   _____

c   carpit   _____

d   mayer   _____

e   discribe   _____

f   chickin   _____

g   vegitable   _____

h   natonal   _____

i   temperary   _____

j   mystory   _____

k   orchistra   _____

l   moterway   _____

Willow's Quest

These five words all contain unstressed vowels. Can you fit them in the word puzzle? The final letter of each word is also the first letter of the next. You can count the letters to help you and the words can go backwards!

literature

formal

library

animal

extra

Add the unicorns sticker to your map.

Letter strings

I'm Aurora. The same letter string can make a different sound in different words. Often, words with the same letter strings can sound quite different.

heart   fear   search   bear

Learning the different sounds that letter strings can make will help you to improve your spelling.

1 Can you sort these words into groups which share the same letter string, even if they don't sound the same? Write them into the correct boxes.

cough	your	field	plough	weight	colour
rumour	tried	height	eight	dough	lie

ough	**our**	**ie**	**eight**

2 Add two words of your own that have the same letter string, and the same sound, as these words.

a **sought** _____ _____

b **stare** _____ _____

c **sight** _____ _____

d **lied** _____ _____

e **dear** _____ _____

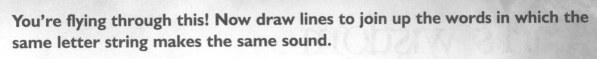

3 You're flying through this! Now draw lines to join up the words in which the same letter string makes the same sound.

a	learn	sour
b	favour	piece
c	niece	earn
d	beard	neighbour
e	hour	might
f	tight	rear

4 Both words in each pair share a letter string that makes a different sound in each word. Find and underline the letter strings.

a	stone	gone	g	through	tough
b	threat	treat	h	few	sew
c	hour	journey	i	heaven	dream
d	notice	rice	j	orange	strange
e	gear	hearth	k	pure	picture
f	bowl	towel	l	great	pleat

Willow's Quest

Change or add one letter to help make each word into the bold word at the end of the line. The first one has been done for you.

a	pie	tie	**tied**
b	soot	_____	**hook**
c	hear	_____	**beard**
d	right	_____	**height**
e	cough	_____	**bought**

Pop the frog sticker on your map.

Pearl's wisdom

1 **Design a poster that explains the different rules for making plurals. Make sure you include examples and illustrations, so that the information is easy to understand.**

Remember to include:
- The rules for adding s and es.
- The rule for most words ending in f.
- The rule for words ending in a consonant followed by y.

2 **Use the magic within you to circle the correctly spelt word in each pair.**

a centre   centur   f freedom   freedum

b factry   factory   g intrest   interest

c primary   primery   h compeny   company

d messinger   messenger   i prepare   prapare

e hospetal   hospital   j heavan   heaven

3 **Look carefully at the letter strings in the box. Find one that could be added to each sum to make new words, then write each complete word again. Many answers are possible for some sums, but use each letter string once.**

> ight   ear   our   ie

a t + _____ = _____

b hon + _____ = _____

c p + _____ = _____

d arm + _____ = _____

e fl + _____ = _____

f flav + _____ = _____

4 **Underline ten mistakes in this piece of text.**

When Pearl is travalling, she always takes lots of photographs with her camra to record her holaday memorys. She loves to show them to her friendes in the Enchanted Forist. Pearl also sends postcards to the animels in the forest, with a special messige for each one. The rabbets love to read about her adventers.

Find the crystals sticker to add to your map.

Nouns

We're Gem and Sparkle. Nouns are words that name things or feelings. There are four types that you need to know about.

Common nouns name ordinary things.

acorn

Proper nouns name specific people, places, the days of the week and the months of the year. They start with capital letters.

Gribbit

Abstract nouns name ideas or feelings.

knowledge

Collective nouns name a group of things.

a herd of cows

⭐ **Wave your wand and underline the nouns in each sentence.**

a   Professor Willow has a lot of knowledge.

b   The squirrel scampered up the tree.

c   A flock of birds flew over the forest.

d   The Enchanted Forest is a magical place.

e   In March the forest is full of bluebells.

f   Red toadstools grew around the tree.

g   Finn lives in a cave in the forest.

h   There was snow on the mountain.

i   Aurora perched on a branch of the tree.

j   The pixies counted fireflies in the trees.

k   Pearl went to visit the foxes.

2 Let's tidy up these nouns by putting them in the correct box.

unicorn   happiness   July   Monday   beetle   Firefly

butterfly   enjoyment   flower   sorrow   understanding   Aurora

common noun	proper noun	abstract noun

3 Now add a suitable collective noun to complete each phrase.

a   a _____ of stairs

b   a _____ of bees

c   a _____ of wolves

d   a _____ of lions

e   a _____ of flowers

f   an _____ of soldiers

Willow's Quest

Solve the clues and then add the nouns to the crossword.

a   a collective noun for a group of sheep

b   an abstract noun often symbolised by a heart

c   the month after September

d   Gribbit's best friend

e   an animal with a black and white stripy face

Add the owl sticker to your map.

Speech

We're Gribbit and Periwinkle. We often want to write down the exact words that our characters say. This is called direct speech and there is special punctuation to help us.

"Hello!" said Sparkle.

At other times, we can describe what characters say without using their exact words. This is called indirect speech.

Sparkle greeted us.

1 **Decide whether each sentence contains direct or indirect speech. Write direct or indirect at the end of each sentence.**

a   Gem wondered where the other fairies were.   _____

b   Professor Willow asked Pearl to sing for him.   _____

c   "Let's have a party!" said Gribbit.   _____

d   Finn explained his idea to the pixies.   _____

e   Sparkle said, "Let's go to the Lake of Wisdom."   _____

2 **Find the direct speech in the sentences below and use it to fill in the speech bubbles.**

Gribbit   Periwinkle

"There are humans in the forest!" panted Gribbit, running in.

Periwinkle asked, "Did they see you?"

"I don't think so," replied Gribbit.

Periwinkle asked, "Where are they now?"

"By the Lake of Wisdom!" said Gribbit.

3 **Let's get busy! Write this indirect speech as direct speech, using the correct punctuation.**

a   Gem asked the other fairies if they wanted to play.

_____

_____

b   Gribbit wondered when the owls' eggs would hatch.

_____

_____

c   Professor Willow told Finn that he would see him later.

_____

_____

d   Aurora said that she had found some new treasures for her nest.

_____

_____

Willow's Quest

Make up your own conversation for these characters. The best pieces of writing contain a mixture of direct and indirect speech. See if you can write at least four sentences including both types of speech.

_____

_____

_____

_____

_____

_____

Find the dragonflies sticker for your map.

Sentences

Using different types of sentences will make your writing more interesting.

> We can sometimes join two short sentences together with a connective.
>
> The rabbit fled because it was afraid.
>
> extra information

> Other times, you can start with a short sentence and add extra information.
>
> The fairies found the pixies, hiding behind a tree.

Whenever you change a sentence, you must make sure that it still makes sense!

1 Read each sentence carefully and put a tick beside those which make sense. No time like the present!

a Professor Willow looked in the Book of Knowledge for.

b The animals gathered to hear Pearl's beautiful singing.

c Hurried across the forest glade because they were late.

d Aurora collects treasures in the forest and keeps them in her nest.

e Sparkle and Gem swirled fairy dust over the flowers.

f Gribbit and Periwinkle in the forest.

2 Choose a sensible piece of extra information to add to each of these sentences. Notice where commas have been used to help the longer sentences make sense.

| in the Book of Knowledge   When night fell   growing by the Lake of Wisdom |

a _____, the owls and bats flew through the trees.

b Pearl found a beautiful flower _____.

c Professor Willow writes _____.

3 Join each pair of sentences together using a connective from the box. Write the new sentence underneath.

then   so   and   but   because

a   The animals sheltered. It was raining.

_____

_____

b   Sparkle looked for Gem. She could not find her.

_____

_____

c   Periwinkle ran into the forest. Gribbit followed him.

_____

_____

d   The squirrel hides his nuts. He can eat them later.

_____

_____

e   Aurora stretched her wings. She flew towards the Mysterious Mountain.

_____

_____

Willow's Quest

Write T for True or F for False by each of these statements.

a   Using different types of sentences makes your writing boring.   _____

b   Connectives are words like and, but or so.   _____

c   You must check that each sentence you write makes sense.   _____

d   You should never add more information to short sentences.   _____

e   Commas can help longer sentences to make sense.   _____

Add the sticker of the woodland picnic to the map.

Verbs

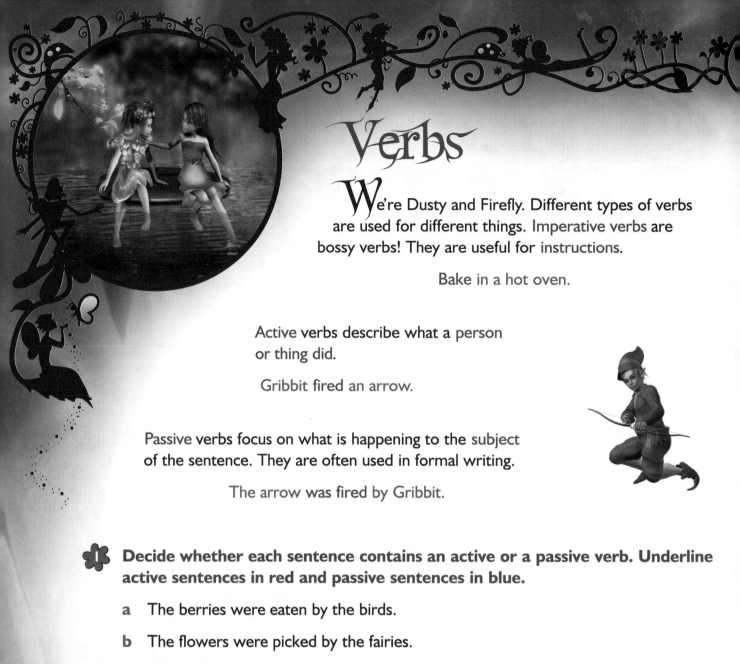

We're Dusty and Firefly. Different types of verbs are used for different things. Imperative verbs are bossy verbs! They are useful for instructions.

Bake in a hot oven.

Active verbs describe what a person or thing did.

Gribbit fired an arrow.

Passive verbs focus on what is happening to the subject of the sentence. They are often used in formal writing.

The arrow was fired by Gribbit.

1 Decide whether each sentence contains an active or a passive verb. Underline active sentences in red and passive sentences in blue.

a The berries were eaten by the birds.

b The flowers were picked by the fairies.

c Pearl sang a beautiful song.

d The guitar was played by Periwinkle.

e Professor Willow unveiled his invention.

f Aurora flew back to her nest.

g The silence was broken with a loud shout.

h Finn visited Pearl by the Lake of Wisdom.

i The moon was hidden by the thick clouds.

j The forest floor was covered by autumn leaves.

k The fairies rested among the flowers.

i Gribbit ate a huge sandwich.

2 Pick suitable imperative verbs from the box to complete Periwinkle's instructions for making a chair out of an acorn cup.

Line   Choose   Remove   Find   Attach   Enjoy

a _____ a large acorn on the forest floor.

b _____ one with a rounded shape.

c _____ the acorn from the cup.

d _____ short twigs to the cup, for legs.

e _____ the cup with tufts of dandelion clock to make a cushion.

f _____ your new chair!

3 Pick a suitable passive verb from the box to complete each sentence.

were stored   were laden   was built   were made   was left

a The message _____ by Aurora.

b The nuts _____ in a hole in a tree.

c A nest _____ at the top of the tree.

d Ripples _____ on the lake by a leaping frog.

e The trees _____ with snow.

Willow's Quest

Decide what kind of verb each sentence contains. Write imperative, active or passive on the line by each sentence.

a Stay on the path in the Enchanted Forest.   _____

b A butterfly landed on the flower.   _____

c The sun broke through the clouds.   _____

d The leaves were blown off the trees.   _____

e The desk was tidied by Professor Willow.   _____

Find the sticker of the bluebells for your map.

17

Pearl's wisdom

1 Complete the chart by adding five of each type of noun.

common nouns	proper nouns	abstract nouns	collective nouns

2 Read these sentences about writing speech and write T for True or F for False.

a When you write the actual words someone says, it is called direct speech.

b Indirect speech is where you describe what someone says, without using their actual words.

c We must use speech punctuation for indirect speech.

d Combining direct and indirect speech carefully can make your writing better.

3 This piece of writing is made up of lots of short sentences. Can you write it again, changing some of the sentences to make it more interesting?

It was snowing in the Enchanted Forest. Professor Willow was reading. He heard a noise outside. He looked out of the window. He was hit in the face by a tiny snowball. It had been thrown by Gribbit!

_____

_____

_____

_____

4 Read this piece of text and then find and underline at least three examples each of imperative, active and passive verbs. Use a different colour for each type of verb.

A postcard was dropped into the Enchanted Forest by a passing bird. It had been addressed to the fairies by Pearl. They all wanted to be the first to read it. "Give it to me!" said Gem, grabbing at the postcard.

"Stop it! I want it!" argued Sparkle, snatching it back.

"Let go!" shouted Dusty, gripping the edge of the card tightly. The fairies pushed and shoved and, in the confusion, the postcard was torn into tiny pieces. The fragments drifted into the Lake of Wisdom where they were gobbled up by a shoal of silvery fish.

"Now we'll never know what it said!" sighed Gem. "What a bunch of pixies we've been!"

5 Write a set of instructions for playing the card game Snap, using imperative verbs.

_____

_____

_____

_____

6 Write a recipe for your favourite ice cream sundae using imperative verbs. Remember to include the ingredients and describe how the sundae is made.

_____

_____

_____

_____

_____

Pop the pearls and shells sticker on your map.

Synonyms

Synonyms are words with similar meanings.

cool   cold   freezing

You can use synonyms to save you from having to repeat the same word in your writing. Understanding the small differences between synonyms can also help you to compare things carefully.

The cool breeze was refreshing, but the freezing rain was a shock!

1 Can you write down a synonym for each word, word warrior?

a   old   _____

b   clever   _____

c   angry   _____

d   jump   _____

e   sleep   _____

f   lose   _____

2 Write these groups of synonyms again, in order of intensity, starting with the least intense.

a   hot   boiling   warm

_____   _____   _____

b   run   jog   sprint

_____   _____   _____

c   drenched   wet   damp

_____   _____   _____

d   pleased   satisfied   delighted

_____   _____   _____

e   angry   furious   annoyed

_____   _____   _____

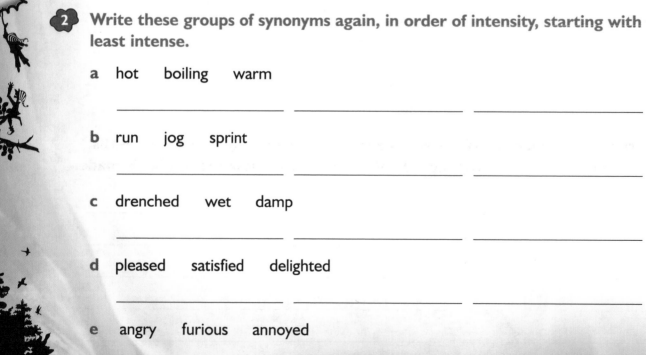

3 When you're writing direct speech, it's very boring to keep using the word said. Pick a different word from the box to complete each of these sentences.

replied   observed   explained   asked   pleaded   suggested

a "Have you seen my hat?" _____ Professor Willow.

b "It's on your head!" _____ Pearl.

c Finn _____ , "Balance is the key to using synonyms."

d "Dusty, please can I borrow your necklace?" _____ Sparkle.

e "There's a storm coming," _____ Gribbit.

f "Let's try some magic?" _____ Firefly.

4 Focus on these words. See if you can find and circle three words that don't belong with the rest.

sad   dejected   unhappy

mischievous

ungrateful   woeful

miserable   irritated   downcast

Willow's Quest

Write down four other words you could use instead of said when you are writing what characters say.

a _____

b _____

c _____

d _____

Add the sticker of the Book of Knowledge.

21

Antonyms

Antonyms are words with opposite meanings.

happy   sad

Many words have no antonyms at all.

gate   garden   write

Some words have just one antonym, but some have more than one!

large   small   tiny   minute   miniature

Antonyms are useful for describing the differences between things.

Sparkle thinks that fairies are pretty and pixies are ugly!

1 **Circle the words that have no antonym. No time like the present!**

dark   early   dirty   eat

buy   greedy   green   jump

2 **Write as many antonyms as you can think of for each of these words.**

a small   _____

b old   _____

c happy   _____

d ill   _____

e slow   _____

f stupid   _____

g rude   _____

h pretty   _____

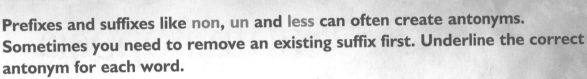

3 Prefixes and suffixes like non, un and less can often create antonyms. Sometimes you need to remove an existing suffix first. Underline the correct antonym for each word.

a	**kind**	nonkind	kindless	unkind
b	**sensible**	unsensible	nonsensible	senseless
c	**believable**	disbelievable	unbelievable	believableless
d	**careful**	careless	uncareful	noncareful
e	**useful**	unuseful	useless	nonuseful
f	**natural**	naturaless	unnatural	nonnatural
g	**reasonable**	unreasonable	nonreasonable	unreason
h	**slip**	unslip	slipless	nonslip
i	**spotty**	unspotty	spotless	nonspotty
j	**fair**	fairless	nonfair	unfair

Willow's Quest

Write these sentences again, choosing antonyms for the bold words. Notice how the meaning of each sentence changes.

a   Gribbit was unhappy because he had a tiny cake.

_____

b   It is light in the forest during the day.

_____

c   Pearl came to visit the old elf.

_____

d   Gem lost her old hat.

_____

Pop the treasure chest sticker on the map.

Onomatopoeia

Onomatopoeia is when words sound like the noise that they describe.

crash   boom   whisper

We can use onomatopoeia to bring our descriptive writing to life, because our readers can easily imagine the sounds.

1   Draw lines to match up the objects with onomatopoeia you could use to describe them.

a   glass breaking   click

b   an egg frying   crunch

c   a light switch   squeak

d   a mouse   squelch

e   walking in mud   sizzle

f   autumn leaves   shatter

2   Use the magic within you to find and underline examples of onomatopoeia in this piece of text.

It had been raining all morning in the Enchanted Forest. Raindrops splashed on to the

leaves and dripped into puddles on the forest floor. The branches of the

trees creaked in the whistling wind, their wet leaves slapping

together. Thunder rumbled in the distance.

3   Use onomatopoeia to describe a woodland walk on a windy autumn day.

_____

_____

_____

_____

4 Write your own onomatopoeia for these objects. Take your time!

a bees

_____

b a door slamming

_____

c a baby crying

_____

d a bonfire

_____

e a balloon bursting

_____

f a hailstorm

_____

g a bird singing

_____

Willow's Quest

Fit these examples of onomatopoeia into the word grid.

wail

groan

rattle

clatter

squelch

Add the sticker of hedgehogs carrying food to the map.

Metaphor and simile

The sky is the limit when you know how to use imagery! Imagery uses writing techniques to paint a picture in your reader's imagination.

Simile is where something is described as if it were something else, using the words as or like.

as pretty as a picture

Metaphor is when you say that something actually is something else.

The berries were jewels.

 Match up the two halves of these well-known similes.

a	as old as	brass
b	as fresh as	a feather
c	swim like	a flash
d	run like	ice
e	as strong as	a mule
f	as cold as	a sheet
g	as bold as	the wind
h	as quick as	day
i	as white as	an owl
j	as light as	an ox
k	as stubbon as	the hills
l	as clear as	a daisy
m	as wise as	a fish

2 Think of your own way to finish each of these similes. Try to be original.

a The unicorn's mane was as soft as _____.

b The Lake of Wisdom was as clear as _____.

c The trees were like _____.

d The stars shone like _____.

e The wind howled like _____.

f Pearl's singing was as sweet as _____.

3 You're flying through this! Now pick a word from the box to complete each metaphor.

blanket   lantern   cotton wool
crystals   mirrors   fingers

a The clouds were _____.

b The moon was a _____.

c The snow was a _____.

d The puddles were _____.

e The twigs were _____.

f The raindrops were _____.

Willow's Quest

Read this piece of text carefully. Underline the similes in red and the metaphors in blue.

In the spring, the forest springs to life. Leaf buds appear like emeralds on the branches. The birds are builders, making cosy nests for eggs like fat pearls. Burrows and dens are nurseries, sheltering baby rabbits, foxes and badgers that soon venture out like explorers.

Put the sticker of a flock of birds on your map.

Pearl's wisdom

1 **Underline the best synonym from the brackets to complete each sentence.**

a The baby rabbits' fur was (doughy / soft).

b Tiny bubbles (burst / shattered) on the surface of the Lake of Wisdom.

c Gem (fell / stumbled) in love with the tiny pair of shoes.

d Aurora (fetches / collects) unusual objects for her nest.

e Professor Willow (spends / pays) hours reading his books.

f A little stream (sprinted / ran) through the clearing.

g Dragonflies' wings are very (delicate / weak).

h Firefly (swept / brushed) Pearl's mane.

2 **Pick a prefix from the box to make antonyms for these words. Then write each word again. Just do your best!**

im   un   in   dis

a polite _____

b tidy _____

c accurate _____

d possible _____

e considerate _____

f agree _____

g appear _____

h true _____

i necessary _____

j practical _____

3 Think of six examples of onomatopoeia for fireworks and add them to the spider diagram. If you can think of any more, add them too!

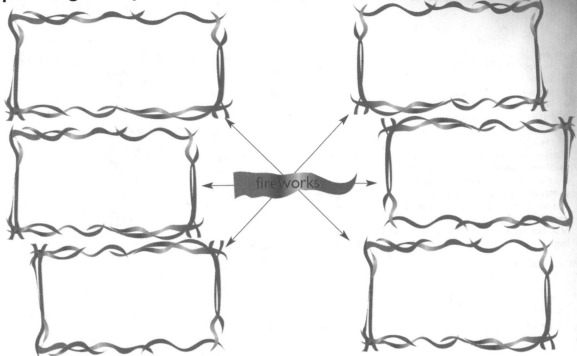

fireworks

4 Write a sentence explaining what you think each simile or metaphor means.

a   The frost was like a carpet of diamonds.

_____

b   The flowerbed was a mosaic of colour.

_____

c   The landscape was a patchwork quilt.

_____

d   The windows were like eyes.

_____

e   The girl had corkscrew hair.

_____

f   The tree's bark was like leather.

_____

Complete your map with the sticker of the mice fishing.

Answers

Pages 2–3

1
a wolves
b loaves
c scarves
d shelves
e cuffs
f selves

2
a fairies
b lorries
c trolleys
d cherries
e donkeys
f jellies

3 plural nouns ending in s: owls, pebbles
plural nouns ending in es: boxes, dishes
plural nouns ending in ves: elves, halves
plural nouns ending in ies: parties, puppies

4 The words that should be underlined are:
pixys, wishs, glovs, webes, berrys.
N.B. The plural of hoof can be spelt either
hoofs or hooves.

Willow's Quest

a	c	i	t	i	e	s	g
d	w	a	j	y	f	e	w
g	b	x	l	i	k	d	o
e	f	r	h	v	m	l	r
t	h	i	e	v	e	s	r
c	s	q	z	o	n	s	i
t	u	a	b	p	c	h	e
v	w	a	t	c	h	e	s

Pages 4–5

1
a jewellery
b miserable
c generally
d factory
e separate
f boundary

2
a Wednesday
b offering
c poisonous
d conference
e frightening
f interest

3 The incorrectly spelt words are: despirate,
diffrence, memrable, deafning, critacise.

4
a remember
b history
c carpet
d mayor
e describe
f chicken
g vegetable
h national
i temporary
j mystery
k orchestra
l motorway

Willow's Quest

f							
o			a	n	i	m	a	l
r			r				i
m			t				b
a			x				r
l	i	t	e	r	a	t	u	r	e
							a
							r
							y

Pages 6–7

1
ough: cough, plough, dough
our: your, colour, rumour
ie: field, tried, lie
eight: weight, height, eight

Pages 2-3 (column 2)

2 Answers will vary, but might include:
a bought — ought
b care — rare
c fight — light
d fried — tried
e fear — gear

3
a learn — earn
b favour — neighbour
c niece — piece
d beard — rear
e hour — sour
f tight — might

4
a one
b eat
c our
d ice
e ear
f ow
g ough
h ew
i ea
j ange
k ure
l eat

Willow's Quest
a tie
b hoot
c bear
d eight
e bough

Pages 8–9

1 Posters will vary, but should include the
different spelling rules specified.

2
a centre
b factory
c primary
d messenger
e hospital
f freedom
g interest
h company
i prepare
j heaven

3 Many answers are possible, but the correct
spellings are:
ight: tight, flight
ear: tear, pear
our: tour, honour, pour, armour, flour,
flavour
ie: tie, pie

4 The words that should be underlined are:
travelling, camra, holaday, memorys, friendes,
Forist, animels, messige, rabbets, adventers.

Pages 10–11

1
a Professor Willow has a lot of knowledge.
b The squirrel scampered up the tree.
c A flock of birds flew over the forest.
d The Enchanted Forest is a magical place.
e In March the forest is full of bluebells.
f Red toadstools grew around the tree.
g Finn lives in a cave in the forest.
h There was snow on the mountain.
i Aurora perched on a branch of the tree.
j The pixies counted fireflies in the trees.
k Pearl went to visit the foxes.

2 common nouns: unicorn, beetle, butterfly,
flower
proper nouns: July, Monday, Firefly, Aurora
abstract nouns: happiness, enjoyment,
sorrow, understanding

Pages 2-3 (column 3)

3 Answers may vary, but the most likely
responses are:
a flight
b swarm
c pack
d pride
e bunch
f army

Willow's Quest

						o							
f	l	o	c	k								
		o		t							b
		v		o							a
		e		b							d
				e							g
p	e	r	i	w	i	n	k	l	e
											r

Pages 12–13

1
a indirect
b indirect
c direct
d indirect
e direct

2
G: There are humans in the forest!
P: Did they see you?
G: I don't think so.
P: Where are they now?
G: By the Lake of Wisdom!

3 Sentences may vary, but might include:
a "Do you want to play?" asked Gem.
b "I wonder when the owls' eggs will
hatch," said Gribbit.
c "I'll see you later, Finn," said Professor
Willow.
d Aurora said, "I've found some new
treasures for my nest."

Willow's Quest
Conversations will vary, but must be correctly
punctuated and include direct and reported
speech.

Pages 14–15

1 The sentences which make sense are: b, d,
e.

2
a When night fell, the owls and bats flew
through the trees.
b Pearl found a beautiful flower growing
by the Lake of Wisdom.
c Professor Willow writes in the Book of
Knowledge.

3
a The animals sheltered because it was
raining.
b Sparkle looked for Gem, but she could
not find her.
c Periwinkle ran into the forest and
Gribbit followed him.
d The squirrel hides his nuts so he can eat
them later.
e Aurora stretched her wings, then she
flew towards the Mysterious Mountain.

Willow's Quest
a False
b True
c True
d False
e True

Pages 16–17

1 a <u>The berries were eaten by the birds.</u>
   b <u>The flowers were picked by the fairies.</u>
   c <u>Pearl sang a beautiful song.</u>
   d <u>The guitar was played by Periwinkle.</u>
   e <u>Professor Willow unveiled his invention.</u>
   f <u>Aurora flew back to her nest.</u>
   g <u>The silence was broken with a loud shout.</u>
   h <u>Finn visited Pearl by the Lake of Wisdom.</u>
   i <u>The moon was hidden by the thick clouds.</u>
   j <u>The forest floor was covered by autumn leaves.</u>
   k <u>The fairies rested among the flowers.</u>
   i <u>Gribbit ate a huge sandwich.</u>
2 a Find
   b Choose
   c Remove
   d Attach
   e Line
   f Enjoy
3 a The message was left by Aurora.
   b The nuts were stored in a hole in a tree.
   c A nest was built at the top of the tree.
   d Ripples were made on the lake by a leaping frog.
   e The trees were laden with snow.

Willow's Quest

a imperative   d passive
b active   e passive
c active

Pages 18–19

1 Answers will vary.
2 a True   c False
   b True   d True
3 Sentences will vary, but might include:
   It was snowing in the Enchanted Forest. Professor Willow was reading when he heard a noise outside. He looked out of the window and was hit in the face by a snowball which Gribbit had thrown!
4 Verbs
   Active verbs
   Passive verbs
   Imperative verbs
   A postcard was dropped into the Enchanted Forest by a passing bird. It had been addressed to the fairies by Pearl. They all wanted to be the first to read it. "Give it to me!" said Gem, grabbing at the postcard. "Stop it! I want it!" argued Sparkle, snatching it back. "Let go!" shouted Dusty, gripping the edge of the card tightly. The fairies pushed and shoved and, in the confusion, the postcard was torn into tiny pieces. The fragments drifted in to the Lake of Wisdom where they were gobbled up by a shoal of silvery fish. "Now we'll never know what it said!" moaned Gem. "What a bunch of pixies we've been!"
5 Answers will vary, but should include imperative verbs.
6 Answers will vary, but should include a description of how to make an ice cream sundae, including the ingredients, using imperative verbs.

Pages 20–21

1 Answers will vary, but might include:
   a ancient   d leap
   b intelligent   e doze
   c furious   f misplace
2 a warm   hot   boiling
   b jog   run   sprint
   c damp   wet   drenched
   d satisfied pleased   delighted
   e annoyed   angry   furious
3 a asked   d pleaded
   b replied   e observed
   c explained f suggested
4 The words that don't belong are: mischievous, ungrateful, irritated

Willow's Quest

Answers will vary, but might include: argued, complained, answered, whispered.

Pages 22–23

1 The words with no antonym are: green, eat, greedy, jump.
2 Answers will vary, but might include:
   a large, big, massive, huge, enormous
   b new, young, fresh, modern
   c unhappy, miserable, sad
   d well, healthy, fit
   e quick, fast, rapid, speedy
   f clever, bright, intelligent, brilliant
   g polite, considerate, helpful
   h plain, unattractive, ugly
3 a unkind   f unnatural
   b senseless   g unreasonable
   c unbelievable   h nonslip
   d careless   i spotless
   e useless   j unfair

Willow's Quest

Sentences will vary, but might include:
a Gribbit was happy because he had a huge cake.
b It is dark in the forest during the night.
c Pearl went to visit the young elf.
d Gem found her new hat.

Pages 24–25

1 a glass breaking   click
   b an egg frying   crunch
   c a light switch   squeak
   d a mouse   squelch
   e walking in mud   sizzle
   f autumn leaves   shatter
2 It had been raining all morning in the Enchanted Forest. Raindrops <u>splashed</u> onto the leaves and <u>dripped</u> into puddles on the forest floor. The branches of the trees <u>creaked</u> in the <u>whistling</u> wind, their wet leaves <u>slapping</u> together. Thunder <u>rumbled</u> in the distance.
3 Answers will vary.
4 Answers will vary, but might include:
   a buzz   e pop
   b bang   f patter
   c howl   g cheep
   d crackle

Willow's Quest

Pages 26–27

1 a as old as   brass
   b as fresh as   a feather
   c swim like   a flash
   d run like   ice
   e as strong as   a mule
   f as cold as   a sheet
   g as bold as   the wind
   h as quick as   day
   i as white as   an owl
   j as light as   an ox
   k as stubborn as   the hills
   l as clear as   a daisy
   m as wise as   a fish
2 Answers will vary.
3 a The clouds were cotton wool.
   b The moon was a lantern.
   c The snow was a blanket.
   d The puddles were mirrors.
   e The twigs were fingers.
   f The raindrops were crystals.

Willow's Quest

In the spring, the forest springs to life. Leaf buds appear like emeralds on the branches. The birds are builders, making cosy nests for eggs like fat pearls. Burrows and dens are nurseries, sheltering baby rabbits, foxes and badgers that soon venture out like explorers.

Pages 28–29

1 a soft   e spends
   b burst   f ran
   c fell   g delicate
   d collects   h brushed
2 a impolite   f disagree
   b untidy   g disappear
   c inaccurate   h untrue
   d impossible   i unnecessary
   e inconsiderate j impractical
3 Answers will vary, but could include: bang, woosh, zoom, fizz, boom, screech.
4 Sentences will vary but might include:
   a The frosty ground sparkled like diamonds because it was covered with tiny ice crystals.
   b The flowerbed was full of different coloured flowers, mixed up like a mosaic.
   c The landscape was full of square fields, each slightly different, which looked like the squares on a huge patchwork quilt.
   d Windows in a building look like eyes, perhaps because the position of the front door makes the front of the house look like a face.
   e The girl's hair was coiled into tight curls which looked like a corkscrews.
   f The tree's bark feels tough and is highly patterned, so that it looks and feels like leather.

Welcome to the Enchanted Forest...

Wonderful work!